Medicine in Britain: He people

Revision Book for GCSE History

By Jack Hartell

Copyright © 2016 by Jack Hartell

All rights reserved. This book or any portion thereof may not be reproduced or used in any manner whatsoever without the express written permission of the publisher except for the use of brief quotations in a book review.

First edition, 2016

This publication is in no way endorsed by any exam board.

I've tried to source only images which are in the public domain, please contact me if I've made a mistake.

Disclaimer

The author can in no way confirm any grade through purchasing and reading this publication.

This publication is best combined with other methods of revision in order to achieve the best grades.

Introduction

"The facts are all there, but without the need to read 2 pages to acknowledge them. This is a must for those struggling with revision as is lighter and refreshing."

"As a revision guide, it can hardly be faulted."

"Small yet very concise. Perfect for GCSE revision."

"I like this because of the clear language and historical detail. It also used the factors format, making it clear what was involved in that time period."

This book is intended for students who are studying the new *Medicine in Britain: Health and the people* (or some variant) GCSE history course. It contains all the knowledge required to achieve good grades, without the waffle that will often crowd lessons and other revision guides. This book features everything you need to know all in one place, so you won't need to go searching through large text books to find any information you may require. I hope this helps you to reach your targets.

Jack Hartell

2016

This book is for the new history courses; it is the follow on from the old 'Medicine through Time' course.

The first few chapters will be useful for gaining some historical context. These first chapters include some of the content from the old medicine through time course to gain an understanding of the key ideas you will need for the new course.

These include ideas from the Ancient Greeks and Ancient Romans, which dramatically shaped medicine for most of European recent history.

Whilst you might not need to learn these by heart, it will be essential understanding Middle Ages and Renaissance medicine.

Contents

ANCIENT GREECE: *DISEASE AND INFECTION*	7
ANCIENT GREECE: *SURGERY AND ANATOMY*	11
ANCIENT GREECE: *PUBLIC HEALTH*	14
ANCIENT ROME: *DISEASE AND INFECTION*	16
ANCIENT ROME: *SURGERY AND ANATOMY*	19
ANCIENT ROME: *PUBLIC HEALTH*	22
PART ONE	
MIDDLE AGES: *DISEASE AND INFECTION*	25
MIDDLE AGES: *SURGERY AND ANATOMY*	32
MIDDLE AGES: *PUBLIC HEALTH*	35
PART TWO	
RENAISSANCE: *DISEASE AND INFECTION*	39
RENAISSANCE: *SURGERY AND ANATOMY*	43
RENAISSANCE: *PUBLIC HEALTH*	49
PART THREE	
INDUSTRIAL REVOLUTION: *DISEASE AND INFECTION*	51
INDUSTRIAL REVOLUTION: *SURGERY AND ANATOMY*	58
INDUSTRIAL REVOLUTION: *PUBLIC HEALTH*	64
PART FOUR	
MODERN TIMES: *DISEASE AND INFECTION*	73
MODERN TIMES: *SURGERY AND ANATOMY*	79
MODERN TIMES: *PUBLIC HEALTH*	85

Ancient Greece: *Disease and Infection*

Another seismic shift was about to occur in Ancient Greece (700-100 BC). With surplus food and wealth, it afforded many people time to study and maybe even become scholars. A new scientific and rational approach had been adopted to all of life, this filtered into medicine. It started with Empedocles' idea of the 4 elements (earth, air, fire and water) in about 560 BC, and it ended in the first fully complete natural theory of the cause of illness - the 4 humours.

Hippocrates was the first great individual in medicine. He was born in Kos (Greek island) in around 460 BC and rejected any supernatural theories concerning health. His most lasting idea was the Hippocratic Oath which is still in use today. It made doctors swear they would do all they could to help their patients, and not work for financial gain. This improved public confidence in doctors.

He stressed the importance of recording and observing patients' symptoms. This allowed many new diseases to be categorised for future reference and made it more likely that doctors would choose the right cure.

He proposed a sequence of actions for a doctor first treating a patient: diagnosis, prognosis, observation and then finally treatment.

Also, the Hippocratic Collection of Books was assembled (how many were actually written by him are unknown); the ideas contained within were used for centuries. He insisted people ate healthily and exercised regularly, and there was still a great emphasis on the important of the individual in looking after themselves. This is an example of a regimen, which was a recommended lifestyle for healthy living. Critics of Hippocrates point out how he focused on treating individuals as just that, individuals. He did not treat specific diseases or illnesses for he believed they were unique to the individual suffering. He thought each patient should be observed, and a treatment plan created based on that person, but not on what illness they had. Many claim Hippocrates also created the 4 humours…

No historian can say for certain who created the 4 humours, but many names have been floated around - Hippocrates or Aristotle, for starters.

It stated that if any of the 4 humours (black bile, yellow bile, blood and phlegm) were out of balance then a person would become ill. The imbalance caused illness. Not the other way round as would be more commonly thought today. If there was too much or too little of one humour then the balance would need to be restored. The most common treatment used by Hippocrates was bleeding. The 4 humours theory was good for spotting disease but added little to actually improving treatment.

Despite the new rational ways of thinking, religion was just as important as ever. The Greek God Asclepius was responsible for health and the Greeks built many great Asclepeions dedicated to him. An Asclepion was an enormous temple for healing - almost the modern day equivalent of a religious *health farm*. They were very popular and by 200BC there was one in every town. If people were ill they may have visited to receive prayer and ceremonial washing and sacrifice from the priest. It was said that during the night Asclepius and his two daughters (Panacea and Hygeia) would visit patients; Asclepius' snake would then *apparently* cure blindness. To advertise the services of the Asclepeion, patients could write inscriptions on walls and often great statues were built in honour of them, and their work.

The Greeks were involved in a large number of wars meaning doctors normally gave common sense treatments for injuries (which stemmed from the battlefield). Also, herbal remedies still formed a major part of treatment.

Summary

- Religion- Asclepia + Asclepius
- Hippocrates: oath, record and observe, a collection of books, 4 humours.
- Emphasis on self- diet and exercise

- Herbal remedies

Factors

INDIVIDUAL GENIUS

RELIGION

TECHNOLOGY

LUCK

Ancient Greece: *Surgery and Anatomy*

Both surgery and anatomy, like in Egypt, had slight improvements. Similarly to in Egypt, metal-working improved. This meant that more precise surgery could be carried out, and as such the lungs of a person with pneumonia could now be drained. Also, there was the discovery that using wine and vinegar on cuts could reduce infection, and therefore death rates (we now know that they're antiseptics). Greeks were also involved in many wars; this gave surgeons plenty of invaluable experience.

Once more, anatomical know-how improved most. Aristotle carried out numerous dissections on animals and encouraged careful observation. Alexandria, a city in Egypt, was founded by Alexander the Great in around 331 BC. This became the centre for medical learning via its library and university. Here, many medics were trained and there was a great translations and book copying centre. This was also mightily important as the only place in the ancient world where human dissections could occur.

Greeks named Herophillus and Erasistratos worked and studied there. Herophillus discovered the difference between the stomach and intestine, the difference between arteries, nerves and veins and the link between heartbeat and pulse. After this, he emphasised the importance of measuring pulse rate.

Erasistratos worked out the different regions of the brain (the cerebrum and the cerebellum) and showed how the nerves and brain are linked. He said nerves were solid and not filled with air – as had previously been thought.

Summary

- Much sharper metals – more precise
- Wine and Vinegar
- War
- Alexandria 331BC
- Herophillus + Erasistratos (differences between stomach + intestines, veins + arteries, pulse + heart rate, brain controlled body)

Factors

LUCK

TECHNOLOGY

WAR

MONEY

GOVERNMENT

INDIVIDUAL GENIUS

Ancient Greece: *Public Health*

Public health was not very good in Ancient Greece. They believed in the importance of a balanced and healthy lifestyle, which fitted in with the belief of the four humours nicely. Greek doctors told their patients not to eat or drink too much; to bath regularly, and exercise frequently. The majority of their ideas were based on Hippocrates' books, but due to the cost of producing them (they had to be handwritten), only the rich were able to afford their own copies. As a result, there were many public bath houses in Greek towns and cities. There were also a few public toilets – but not very many.

However, towns were extremely crowded, and only an extremely basic sewer system existed. Much like the Egyptians, the government left the people to keep themselves clean – and their streets. As a result, they were extremely dirty – causing many epidemic diseases such as outbreaks of plague. As mentioned previously, Asclepeions (Ancient Greek equivalent of a *Health Farm)* provided a place for treatment.

There was very much an economic divide. The rich could afford their own baths, and maybe even water supply, whereas the poor would have lived in squalor.

Summary

- Asclepia
- Emphasis on self
- Streets dirty
- Crowded
- Hippocrates – diet and exercise
- No sewers

Factors

GOVERNMENT

MONEY

RELIGION

INDIVIDUAL

Ancient Rome: *Disease and Infection*

Religion was still just as important in Ancient Rome as it was in Ancient Greece. During the Antonine Plague (Galen's Plague) from AD 165-180, Ancient Romans turned back to the Greek God Asclepius (for no cures were working) – who remained a central God until the end of the Roman era. Many temples were built which were dedicated to the Gods of healing

Taking a step backwards in time from the Antonine Plague, Romans thought themselves better than the Greeks so initially rejected any Greek ideas. Greek doctors were even imprisoned (despite the majority of Rome's doctors being Greek) which resulted in a generally low status for the medical profession. The head of the family was in charge of medicine and they used common sense remedies and conducted religious rituals. More advanced herbal remedies were used because more herbs / spices could be obtained from the wide Roman Empire. This all changed, however, in 46BCE when Julius Caesar made all Greek doctors Roman citizens. This allowed the one other great individual doctor of the ancient times to take centre stage…

Claudius Galen drew the work of all the ancient doctors and scholars together as well as adding some new ideas of his own. He developed the 4 humours theory (and was the first to introduce it to Rome) to improve the treatments it provided. He created the '*opposites theory*' which stated that if someone has a cold illness (such as a cold or flu) use a hot treatment (like a chilli). If someone was very hot (like with a fever) use cold cures (such as a cucumber). Like Hippocrates, he too encouraged exercise and a healthy diet. His ideas and books became the central medicinal guides for centuries afterwards. His theories spread quickly as for a large part of his working life he was a doctor to the emperor. He was very influential for thousands of years.

Overall, very little actually changed in Ancient Rome for Roman medicine was really just a continuation of Greek ideas and practices.

Summary

- Religion important- Galen Plague prayed to Asclepia.
- Galen: opposites theory. Wrote books – introduced 4 humours.
- Large temples
- Diet and exercise
- Herbal remedies

Factors

GOVERNMENT

INDIVIDUAL GENIUS

RELIGION

LUCK

Ancient Rome: *Surgery and Anatomy*

As in *disease and infection,* Roman surgery was very similar to that of the Greeks – it continued their success. Surgery improved slightly for now opium was used as a mild anaesthetic. In addition, there was a new antiseptic: turpentine.

Some new surgery was now carried out, this included being able to remove bladder stones and cataracts. The enormous Roman army provided lots of practice for surgeons meaning new battlefield techniques developed. There were special Roman army hospitals called Valetudinaria.

Surgeons were supposed to be young with a strong hand and had to be able to ignore patients' screams!

Pedanius Dioscorides wrote 5 encyclopaedias on the subject of herbal medicines and drugs which were read for more than 1500 years. The collective name for them was *De Materia Medica*.

As with previous times, anatomical knowledge improved more than surgical. Again, Claudius Galen was pivotal in the new discoveries. He trained at Alexandria and then became a doctor to gladiators; he learned much about human anatomy through gladiator wounds. Later, as he gained influence, he began encouraging dissection. However, there were not enough human bodies available and he turned to using apes instead. He firmly believed that all of the parts of the human body were perfect and that each part had a specific role to play. He proved that speech was controlled by the brain – not the heart – and showed that both veins and arteries carry blood. He did public demonstrations of his knowledge and in one much-recounted episode he systematically cut the spinal nerves of a pig. When he cut a specific one the pig ceased squealing – this showed that the nerves were responsible for controlling certain bodily functions.

However, as one might expect when examining apes, Galen made mistakes. For example, he said that the human jaw bone is made from two bones when in fact it's just one. He believed that the liver secreted new blood for the heart - this does not occur - and he got the shape of the liver wrong. Finally, he thought that rete mirabile (which are blood vessels on the base of the brain) were found in both humans and animals. In fact, they are only in the brains of animals.

Summary

- War
- Mild anaesthetic – opium
- Galen – public demonstrations (pig – nerves in spine), trained in gladiator hospital

Factors

TECHNOLOGY

WAR

INDIVIDUAL GENIUS

RELIGION

Ancient Rome: *Public Health*

The Roman public health system was a seismic shift in terms of public health in the Ancient world. Prior to the Roman period, absolutely no effort had been made by governments and rulers to care for the health of its people. There were a few reasons for the changes in Roman public health, for example, the army needed to be kept healthy, the Romans realised that dirt equals disease, the Government was rich and powerful (could afford highly skilled engineers) and a general distrust in Greek methods (who believed in no government intervention).

The first, and perhaps best, change was to build all towns and cities in relatively clean and safe places. This meant not near marshes, swamps or polluted and dirty water. Attempts were then made to keep these towns (and army forts) free of disease; clean.

In every town and city, bath houses were built. Anybody could use them and they were very cheap. Reservoirs were created and aqueducts built to transfer this fresh spring water into the towns / cities. Once there, water pipes transported the water into important buildings, some homes (of the most influential people) and all public fountains and pumps. Large sewers were then built to remove any human waste – most towns had toilets built directly over the sewers.

However, there were many major flaws. Public baths were the perfect breeding ground for all number of diseases, which easily spread from person to person in the confined space, for they weren't emptied regularly enough (only once a week). The sewers were too large (waste didn't flow away quickly enough), were open air (smell and germs spread), were made of rough stone (trapped bacteria) and often emptied into rivers used for washing. The water pipes were made of lead which caused lead poisoning. Finally, the rich benefitted more (had own water supply) and the poor still lived in terribly crowded and dirty conditions – where waste was just thrown onto the streets. All of this meant that plague still occurred (for example Galen's Plague AD165).

Large towns and cities were still overcrowded, and the good transport systems and widespread army meant disease spread very quickly.

Summary

- Realised dirt = disease
- Baths, reservoirs, aqueducts, water pipes, sewers, public toilets
- Flaws – still plague

Factors

GOVERNMENT

MONEY

TECHNOLOGY

WAR

PART ONE

Middle Ages: *Disease and Infection*

In a period named the Dark Ages (500AD – 1000AD) medicine, and all of civilised society, saw an enormous decline. In around 500AD the Western Roman Empire collapsed, and numerous tribes (Vikings, Saxons...) took over Europe. The tribes spent their money on war, and had no interest in medicine, health or new scientific discovery - they even burnt many of the ancient texts on medicine. However, some were preserved in the East Roman Empire or Byzantine Empire in Constantinople (modern day Istanbul).

Now there existed strong beliefs in superstition, and a return to a completely supernatural approach to medicine. Many cures involved prayer, but some herbal remedies (passed down the generations) existed as the only natural treatments. Any new ideas would not have spread as war had severely disrupted travel and trade routes.

Islamic Empire

However, the Islamic Empire (700AD-1450AD) was far more advanced than Europe at this time. Doctors and scholars had been pushed out of Jerusalem and settled in Persia (modern day Iran). There, they began translating the ancient Greek and Roman texts into Arabic (the most famous Arab to do this was Hunain ibn Ishaq) meaning the medical knowledge of the Islamic Empire was far greater than in Europe where many texts had been lost.

There was one strong leader (of stark contrast to in Europe) who spent on education and health. Hospitals opened because the Qur'an instructed them to care for those who were ill. For probably the first time, doctors had to pass an exam to obtain a license in order to practise (this occurred from 931AD onwards). Additionally, alchemy (like *chemistry* – trying to turn base metals into gold) developed which meant new techniques (such as distillation) were discovered to create drugs. All major cities had public baths and piped water.

There were two main individuals in the Arabic world at this time: Al Rhazi and Ibn Sina (or Avicenna). Al Rhazi followed Hippocrates by encouraging careful observations of symptoms. He was also impressed by Galen but importantly was prepared to criticise him. He was the first to recognise the difference between measles and smallpox.

Ibn Sina wrote a 1,000,000 word encyclopaedia (called The Canon of Medicine) which summarised almost all of medicine up until 1000AD; it included Galen, Hippocrates,

Islamic doctors and his own ideas. It also contained within it the properties of more than 750 drugs and plants. He created tension amongst scholars at this time because he seemingly went against orthodox Islam by claiming God was not interested in individuals and that the soul was not eternal. To make this worse, he did not subscribe to the creation story and he was often condemned for having an interest in Greek philosophers.

These ideas slowly began to seep into Europe throughout the 12th century, partly due to the Christian crusades which attempted to restore Christendom to the *Holy Lands* in and around Jerusalem (currently under the power of the Islamic Empire). The amount of trade conducted between Europe and the Middle East also began to increase, further allowing ideas to spread.

European Middle Ages (1000AD – 1450AD)

This period is characterised by the supreme control of the Catholic Church, this only heightened the superstitions from the dark ages. All scholars were Catholic, all teaching was done in church institutions and the most educated were normally employed in some sort of church role. This meant the church had incredible power when it came to dictating how medicine and treatments would work.

The church hindered the progress of medicine in many ways. They only allowed Galen and Hippocrates to be read. This was because they felt if the ancient texts were questioned then maybe the Bible would be, too, and additionally because of Galen's view that every part of the human body had a specific purpose (which fitted in with the view that God created humans perfectly). The main reason he Galen was encouraged, though, was that he did not stress the polytheistic side of Roman culture in his work, therefore (unintentionally) not offending the monotheistic Christian and Islamic churches and scholars. However, many of the ancient texts were lost so translations were often incorrect or had major sections missing.

The church, obviously, encouraged that God caused disease which of course worsened treatments, although they did set-up, run and pay for many universities and hospitals (for example, St Bartholomew's).

Doctors followed the 4 humours theory, and relied on treatments including bleeding, using herbal remedies and checking the colour of urine against a chart. The belief in the ancient ways was so strong that it was firmly believed it was better to be well read in the art of Roman and Greek medicine than to actually have any practical experience.

They used zodiac charts (which determined the position of planets) to work out what was wrong with a patient or to decide the right time to operate on a particular body part.

However, ordinary people could not afford to pay for a doctor, so instead turned to local monks, apothecaries (who provided drugs), barber-surgeons (who were untrained and risky) or wise women – who used traditional herbal remedies.

From the 10th century, women were able to train as doctors because of the Laws of King Edgar. However, as the medical profession became more specialised by the 1300s, it became a male only career. Universities had started offering medical training and guilds were formed, for example, the Guild of Surgeons.

The Black Death (1348)

The Black Death was most probably a combination of the bubonic and pneumonic plagues which decimated European populations by up to 60% in and just after 1348.

Both variations of plague were spread by rats and fleas and came into Europe from the Far East (China) via trade ships. The bubonic plague causes enormous swellings to form (called buboes) primarily under the armpits and in the groin area killing 2/3 sufferers within four days. The pneumonic plague is very similar, however instead causes a lung infection. Many patients die within just a day and a half of contracting the disease.

In general, people had absolutely no clue as to why it was infecting so many, so to stop its spread they attempted to clean the streets (organised by King Edward III in England) and burn herbs (to prevent miasma - the idea that bad air and smell caused disease); doctors bled and purged people (to restore the balance of humours), checked urine and, according to John of Burgundy (a writer about the plague) were encouraging people not to eat and drink too much. Desperation led people in some countries to blame the Jews for poisoning the water supply.

Other supernatural theories also existed. For example, the position of the planets was blamed. Alternatively, many believed God had sent the pestilence (as it was then called) as a punishment. Because of this, flagellants walked the streets whipping themselves in order to repent their sins. Magic spells were chanted and large (human size) candles were lit to ward off spirits. In Barcelona, a 7km long candle was lit to protect the city. Many thought this would be the end of the world.

Summary

- Church dominance – Galen + Hippocrates
- Decline
- Church set-up universities, and hospitals in monasteries
- No real ideas about Black Death 1348

Factors

LUCK

RELIGION

WAR

INDIVIDUAL GENIUS

Middle Ages: *Surgery and Anatomy*

Surgery and anatomy did not necessarily decline as much as *disease and infection* during the Middle Ages, but certainly no meaningful progress was really made. In the early 1300s, a new anaesthetic called hemlock was discovered.

However, surgeons had lost respect and were looked down upon by doctors (who studied anatomy). Many were actually untrained barber-surgeons (yes, they did also cut hair!).

Hugh and Theodoric di Lucca first argued that pus in a wound was not a good thing – they went on crusade together in 1214. Previously, doctors thought pus was "praiseworthy" and its appearance in a wound was a positive sign. They were also two of the first to notice wine's antiseptic qualities.

Later, Henry de Mondeville, a military surgeon, taught (and wrote a book) that one should clean and close a wound, attempting to prevent pus from forming. He also suggested that Galen was not always right and that surgeons should try and experiment more, to find out new things.

As well as practical experience, many surgeons could learn from books from both the ancient and the medieval period. Roger of Salerno composed the first European textbook in the 12th century and Guy de Chauliac wrote Chirurgia Magna (Great Surgery) – although this was dedicated to Galen, Hippocrates and the great Islamic doctors, and it did not really contain his own ideas.

John of Ardene is often considered the father of modern surgery. He strived to find actual working cures of which many are still used today. Many of his treatments stemmed from his involvement with the army during the 100 Years War, or concerned the treatment of injuries sustained from horse-riding (for everyone had to do this to travel anywhere). He believed the rich should pay for his services, but he worked for the poor for free.

Again many wars gave plenty of opportunity for battlefield surgeons. Zodiac charts formed a major part of a surgeon's armoury telling them when and sometimes where to operate.

Anatomy did not change. Initially, the Catholic Church banned dissection, but later allowed one per year (on a convicted criminal). However, this was only done in order to prove that Galen was correct. If Galen's ideas and the test body did not match then they thought the body must have been wrong! Students would learn through hearing a lecturer or surgeon reading through Galen's books whilst completing a dissection.

Summary

- Church control – dissections banned
- Later allowed 1 per year – only to prove Galen correct
- Surgeons looked down upon – doctors studied anatomy
- Mild anaesthetics
- War
- Zodiac Chart

Factors

LUCK

RELIGION

Middle Ages: *Public Health*

Here there was an astonishing decline. Any facilities built by the Romans fell into disrepair because all the skilled engineers had left and some tribes even intentionally destroyed public service buildings. Leaders spent available funds on war (and staying in power) rather than on public health. This resulted in life expectancy decreasing, infant mortality rate increasing, an increase in the number of women dying in childbirth, more bone disease, more waste on the streets and more polluted water supplies. This was further worsened by the fact that many people had their livestock living in their homes *with* them.

This slowly began to improve in the UK in the 11th century. During the Norman Conquest of 1066, many homes and building were destroyed by fire. They were rebuilt to a much higher standard – stone - and with separate accommodation for animals. Other changes occurred over the next few hundred years, for example, butchers were forced to operate in separate areas of towns, cess pits were lined with stone whilst more importantly being emptied regularly and wells were dug to reach fresh water supplies.

Fines were issued for dropping waste and groups of *rakers* (street cleaners) were employed to clean up the existing mess on the streets. However, the English monarchy was not wealthy enough throughout this period to enforce these new laws and, as such, they were regularly ignored.

Apart from this, the monarch did not involve himself in public health affairs, instead, this was left to local corporations fronted by powerful men who didn't want to pay the higher taxes needed to fund any public health improvements. The monarch felt health and medicine were *below* him; instead, it was his duty to deal with war, and other brave, admirable and honourable past times. Furthermore, due to the incredibly strong religious beliefs, people didn't worry about dirt. They felt all disease was sent by God, so keeping clean wouldn't affect them in any way.

At this time, Monasteries provided the best health care. They had sewers, water pipes and toilets built in. This was partly due to the wealth and power of the Catholic Church in Europe during the Middle Ages. Ordinary people would often have gone to monasteries to receive food packets and sometimes simple remedies.

The increasing number of wars were responsible for many public health issues. During times of unrest, people opted to live within a city's walls, which led to overcrowding, whilst longer sieges would have led to mass starvation. Travelling soldiers would have carried disease with them, spreading it wherever they went.

Black Death 1348

As previously mentioned, the Black Death was likely a combination of bubonic and pneumonic plagues which killed up to 60% of Europe's population. Some natural approaches to preventing the disease were made, for instance in England, King Edward III ordered streets to be cleaned, people carried herbs and perfumes (by virtue of the miasma theory) and pressed chickens against sores to draw pus out, whilst others tried to squeeze their buboes (large inflammations under the armpits and in the groin area). Supernatural *treatments* still existed which included praying, using magic and relying upon the zodiac (the position of the planets).

Summary

- Decline – rulers = war and no interest
- 1066 slight increase – new stone houses
- Black Death – miasma / God – streets cleaned, but no money

Factors

WAR

LUCK

MONEY

GOVERNMENT

RELIGION

PART TWO

Renaissance: *Disease and Infection*

The very word *renaissance* means *rebirth*, and that's exactly what occurred in this period. There was a rebirth of ancient ways of thinking. Not much in terms of medicine changed, but there was definitely a shift in attitude from a conservative to an inquisitive one amongst doctors and scholars. The roots of this could even be claimed to be the Black Death. Following the Black Death, survivors were better off (as they could claim higher wages), and could, therefore, devote more time and money to education.

Another big shift came as the result the Fall of Constantinople, modern day Istanbul, in 1453. This helped to recover many of the ancient texts which were lost in the Middle Ages, because many of the eastern scholars, trained in ancient ways, migrated west from Turkey into mainland Europe. This also aided in reviving an interest in learning and discovery which brought with it a renewed vigour in the belief of the 4 humours and opposites theory. The Scientific Revolution, also happening at this time, created more interest in experimentation. In 1660 the Royal Society was founded;

this was an important institution in encouraging new scientific discovery. It helped the conservative attitudes persisting from the Middle Ages to slowly die away.

To highlight the new mindset, the bezoar stone story from France is useful. King Charles of France was recommended to use a bezoar stone (from an animal similar to a goat) to treat all poisons. His surgeon Paré (who will be discussed in much greater detail later) informed him this could not be so. It was tested on a live 'victim' who was first given a deadly poison and then had the bezoar stone treatment used on him. He died – the stone did not work - but at least they were experimenting and trying out new things.

In 1454, the printing press was invented by Johannes Gutenberg. This sped up the spreading of new ideas and drastically reduced the cost of producing books (for previously they were copied up by hand by monks). However, this did not lead to an increase in literacy levels amongst the poor as there was still no formal education and the books were still far too expensive.

The new printing press helped a certain man named Martin Luther. He essentially started a new church – the Protestant church – in Germany. This was the beginning of the period known as the Reformation, and it occurred in Britain too when Henry VIII turned away from Catholicism and the Pope. This started a period which allowed for more open debate about ideas; even leading to Galen being challenged.

Paracelsus was one such individual who disputed Galen. He was from Switzerland and insisted on observing for oneself rather than having a reliance on ancient texts. He believed his ideas better than that of Ancient Rome, and to show it he publically burned Galen's books.

He held the belief cures should be made from chemicals; often this was chemicals from plants. This was a pioneering opinion. He believed in balance, like Hippocrates, but of a different kind. A balance between minerals and elements in the body, and nature and the stars. Human health, therefore, depended on balance both inside and outside the body. He thought God had sent him messages regarding the medicinal quality of plants by their shape. He lectured in German (rather than Latin) so he could be easily understood by the laymen. A lot of his work was concerned with fairies and pixies, so consequently he was, by and large, ignored as people thought him completely mad!

In England, increased trade and travel allowed new ingredients to be used from abroad, this included rhubarb, (for the bowels and, less favourably, tobacco and opium.

Thomas Sydenham became known as the *English Hippocrates*. He was of a new breed of doctor more interested in the scientific method. Unlike many of his contemporaries and predecessors, he valued direct observations of his patients as opposed to learning from a book. His main book *Observationes Medicae* became a core book from which students were able to learn. He was one of the pioneers of a classification system for disease, which helped in diagnosis.

Summary

- Reduction in church power
- Galen questioned by Paracelsus (although he was a bit mad!)

Factors

RELIGION

LUCK

INDIVIDUAL GENIUS

Renaissance: *Surgery and Anatomy*

Similarly to *disease and infection*, there was not much change in *surgery and anatomy* in the Renaissance. As in the Middle Ages, there were three main types of surgery undertaken: trephining (still!), amputations and removing tumours. Although, there were some minor alterations to battlefield surgery because of a surgeon named Ambroise Paré.

He was a French barber-surgeon in the 1500s and was called up to the French Army by Francis I to fight at Piedmont (in Italy). There, by chance, he changed the way gunshot wounds were treated. This was important because high powered guns had just been introduced to warfare.

The norm had been to pour boiling oil onto wounds in order to cauterise. But one day he ran out of oil, so instead he used an old Roman recipe comprised of turpentine, egg white and oil of roses. The next day he checked all the patients fully expecting those with the new mixture to have died. However, on the contrary, he discovered those treated with the hot oil were in great pain whilst his patients treated with the Roman recipe were not only alive but in considerably less discomfort. It's important to point out, though, that the implementation of this new technique did not occur for many, many years after Paré had died.

Paré also introduced using ligatures to battlefield surgery. This involved tying together individual arteries to prevent blood loss instead of pressing a red-hot iron to the cut – where many patients died of the extreme pain. It's important to note he did not invent this method, but instead, it was first described by the Arab doctors several centuries earlier. This may have actually increased the death rate because now it took longer for the surgeon to close the wound, thus increasing the chance of an infection.

His two methods dramatically reduced the pain patients felt, however, they were largely ignored by the medical community as surgeons stuck to more traditional methods. He wrote many books: *Methods of Treating Wounds, Works on Surgery, The method of curing wounds caused by arquebus and firearms* and *Treatise on Surgery.* He also contributed to work on prosthetic limbs.

The most important advancement in the Renaissance was in the knowledge of anatomy. Many factors contributed to this improvement (some already mentioned). There was a reduction in Catholic Church power meaning more dissections could occur and Galen could be challenged. Also, the new scientific study amounted to more interest in the discovery and research of the human body.

The printing press ensured books could be produced quicker and cheaper, and crucially without mistakes. Finally, new artistic techniques were developed because artists wanted more realistic drawings – as art became more popular. This produced more accurate books from which to learn from and new individuals such as Leonardo da Vinci to bridge the gap between science and art. He was known as a Renaissance Man; this was someone well educated in both science and art who would have seen no obvious distinction between the two fields.

Andreas Vesalius was a Dutch physician working in Italy. He studied the human body himself and did not rely on Galen. It's often claimed that he used to steal the bodies of criminals to examine and dissect them. His book, *On the Fabric of the Human Body* (released in 1543), was an extremely detailed account (including large pictures) of all parts of the body – both inside and out. In terms of modern standards, it was very accurate. It was read across Europe. One of his other books *Tabulae Sex* was also influential.

Importantly, he noticed some of Galen's mistakes. This was very brave for at this time a physician could have his licence removed for going against the work of the ancients. He challenged Galen on the makeup of the human jaw bone; he realised it was one bone when Galen had incorrectly taught it was two. Vesalius showed that the septum in the middle of the heart has no tiny holes in it, also as Galen had incorrectly believed.

Vesalius thought that the practice of bleeding patients should stop, but this was ignored because of the old Islamic texts which said it should happen, and from the still strong belief in the four humours. His work challenged the accepted stance of following Galen; it began to prove to doctors that there was more to medicine than just the writings of a man living two millennia ago.

William Harvey was another anatomist; he lived in London in the 1600s, and he was very interested in the heart. Harvey, by careful examination and dissection of lizards, proved the heart is a pump. The inspiration of this is often claimed to be the water pumps in London. He also showed how the volume of blood in the body always remains constant which means it's not continuously used up and remade, and that blood circulates the body in just one direction.

This challenged Galen's views about the heart and arteries (especially how Galen believed blood moved through the heart as he thought there were invisible pores inside the heart through which blood flows). Despite showing the levels of blood remain the same and thus opposing the 4 humours theory, he still continued to bleed patients to cure them which shows even he had no conviction in his revolutionary ideas. He wrote a book, *On the Motion of Heart and Blood* (released in 1628), about his findings.

However, many refused to believe these two individuals because they couldn't believe Galen might be wrong.

Additionally, neither of them actually saved any lives at the time, but they did provide a good theoretical framework for future surgical work.

On a final side note, in England in 1518, the Royal College of Physicians was set up by Henry VIII. It was able to control who was able to work officially as a doctor, prospective doctors had to pass an oral exam.

Summary

- Slowly starts improving – church control decreases allows more dissections. 3 types: trephining, tumours and amputations
- Pare: gunshot wounds – mixture (turpentine) and ligature = reduced pain
- Scientific study resumes
- Art techniques = realistic drawings
- Printing Press 1454
- Vesalius: A Fabric on the Human Body. Corrected Galen (jawbone and heart).
- Harvey: challenged Galen on heart – proved was heart and blood circulated in one direction. Wrote book.

Factors

LUCK

TECHNOLOGY

RELIGION

ART

Renaissance: *Public Health*

There is very little knowledge required again – it remained very similar to as it was during the Middle Ages. The only specific details needed are that of the Great Plague of 1665...

This was an identical combination of diseases to the Black Death, but 300 years later. This suggested that no real public health advancements had been made. Although, the actual outbreak *was* better dealt with; the fact it never left London is proof of this. Examiners were appointed to find the cause of death of people and anybody who'd had the plague had their house locked up and a red cross placed on the door. Relatives were quarantined for a month, with watchmen to ensure nobody left. The dead were buried at least 6 feet deep to prevent contact, and public entertainment was banned. Other countries' strict import laws (keeping ships quarantined for 40 days) may have also reduced the spread of the disease across Europe.

Thus far, war has generally been seen to advance medicine. However, this was not always the case. In the Thirty Years War (1618-1648) soldiers and refugees spread the plague which killed millions. It took more than two centuries for Germany to recover.

Summary

- Same – same plague came back
- Better dealt with – didn't leave London – Government more involved (banned entertainment etc...)

Factors

LUCK

RELIGION

GOVERNMENT

PART THREE

The Industrial Revolution:
Disease and Infection

N ow, training at universities was based on natural ideas, with observation, recording and experimentation strongly encouraged. Probably as a consequence, d*isease and* infection improved on an unimaginable scale between 1750 and 1900.

To prevent disease there was a new method called inoculation. Originating from China, it was brought to Western Europe, from Turkey, by Lady Mary Wortley Montagu.

It involved taking the pus from someone with a weak strain of smallpox and covering a needle in it. Then this needle would be drawn through a small cut in someone being inoculated. This would then essentially immunise someone against smallpox. However, it was quite dangerous – patients often contacted the full disease and died – and the pathogen was still highly contagious, so a person inoculated could infect many others with the very illness they were trying to prevent in the first instance. It was a big business and many could not afford it, but a better preventative measure was on the horizon: vaccination.

Edward Jenner was a doctor working in the Gloucestershire countryside in the late 1700s. He was investigating smallpox when he noticed that the milkmaids who caught cowpox never caught the much more deadly smallpox.

He decided to test theory scientifically. First, he trawled back through all the medical records and confirmed no farmer or milkmaid had ever caught both. Next, he decided to actually test this theory out on a person. In 1796, he injected 8-year-old James Phipps with cowpox, and then after it had passed gave him smallpox. There was no reaction; the boy had not caught smallpox. He tried it on 23 more test subjects, all of which were successful. In 1798 he published his report called *An Enquiry into the Causes and Effects of Variolæ Vaccinæ known by the Name of Cowpox* naming his discovery vaccination after the Latin *vacca* meaning cow.

There was a lot of opposition to his vaccination with even an Anti-Vaccine League being established in 1866. People were worried about having an animal disease injected into them, and some doctors didn't take as much care as Jenner meaning some patients died. Some still believed smallpox was a punishment for sin with the only cure being prayer. Even the Royal Society refused to publish his book - claiming it was too revolutionary. The old method of inoculation also made many doctors a lot of money and these doctors were especially against vaccination.

However, the UK Government was in support, and they donated £30,000 to Edward Jenner to support his work, the US President endorsed it and Napoleon had the whole French army vaccinated. In 1852, vaccination was made compulsory in the UK.

The smallpox infection rate dramatically decreased and it was eradicated worldwide in 1980. In the UK the decline of smallpox can also be attributed to public health reforms in the late 19th century. As Jenner did not know how his vaccination worked, it was difficult for others to learn from his discovery.

The next great discovery occurred between 1861 and 1864: Germ Theory from Louis Pasteur (a Frenchman). From the 17th century, scientists had been able to see microorganisms (courtesy of Anthony van Leuwenhoek's microscope). The scientists believed they were created because of spontaneous generation – rotting things just randomly turned into microorganisms. It was because of this that they thought disease and decay caused germs.

Pasteur disagreed, he thought germs caused disease and decay (as is thought today). He was then able to prove his hypothesis correct through a series of experiments. Initially, he took two bottles of water, one sealed and one unsealed. After a period of time, the sealed one had no bacteria in it, but the unsealed one did. This proved that germs did not form from spontaneous generation, but instead were from the air. He used this first for the alcohol industry. Alcoholic drinks were going sour, and when looking at them under a microscope he saw two different types of bacteria – one in non-sour alcohol and the other in sour alcohol (showing that a certain bacteria *did* cause the decay).

Then he was asked by the French Government to help milk selling businesses and he was subsequently able to prove that heating milk killed the bacteria, the product of which is now known as Pasteurised milk. He thought germs in the air caused disease and decay, but he was ridiculed for this belief.

In 1864 he completed a set of public experiments to prove himself right. For his next piece of scientific work, he showed how germs in the air spread disease amongst silk worms. In 1865 his daughter died of cholera, this made him determined to investigate human germs next. He took an air sample from a cholera hospital ward and analysed its contents; however, he wasn't able to distinguish between the different bacteria present.

It was a man named Robert Koch (German) who made the first proper inroads into human disease. Between 1873 and 1875 he showed how germs make a wound go septic and later managed to identify the specific bacterium that caused some human diseases, namely anthrax and septicaemia in 1878. To make this easier, he developed methods of staining and growing bacteria so that they could be photographed under a microscope. From this, other scientists managed to *see* other human disease causing pathogens.

Now, heightened by the Franco – Prussian (Germany) wars between 1870 -1871, there was a fierce rivalry between Pasteur and Koch. This helped them, for the French and German Governments began investing heavily in Pasteur and Koch respectively because of national pride. Pasteur, determined to beat Koch, hired more assistants and began aiding farmers with regard to a chicken cholera epidemic (between 1878 and 1881). Charles Chamberland, one of Pasteur's workers, had a jar of the chicken cholera which he was meant to inject into some chickens. However, he forgot and went on holiday. When he came back he saw the jar and injected the chickens as he was originally supposed to. To his amazement, they did not contract cholera. He informed Pasteur, and was told to infect them with a new set of cholera bacteria – the chickens did not contract cholera again. He had created a new vaccine. Later, Pasteur proved how weakened bacteria could act as a vaccine, which explained how Jenner's smallpox vaccination worked. From this discovery, he was able to create the vaccine for anthrax.

Koch worked hard from 1881 to find two new human bacteria: tuberculosis and cholera. But it was Pasteur who received the limelight again for creating the first vaccine for rabies. He tested it on Joseph Meister in 1885 – and it worked.

Meanwhile, they were aided by a man named Fredrich Löffler. After Edwin Klebs had found the diphtheria bacterium in 1883, Löffler cultivated them and was led to believe they made people ill because they released toxins into the body. This was proved to be a correct hypothesis by Pierre-Emile Roux in the same year. The first antitoxin to be produced was in 1891 by Emil von Behring.

Summary

- University = natural theories
- Edward Jenner = doctor in the countryside. Milkmaids did not get smallpox if they caught smallpox. 1796 James Phipps. 1798 Report on his vaccination.
- 1861 – Louis Pasteur Germ Theory – working for alcohol, silk and dairy industry proves germ = decay / disease. 1865 daughter dies.
- 1878, Robert Koch discovers bacteria responsible for anthrax via new staining and photographing technique, the creation of agar jelly.
- 1878-81 = LP discovers how vaccination works = farming industry – chicken cholera.
- 1881-82 = RK – TB and Cholera bacteria
- 1885 = LP vaccination against rabies

Factors

LUCK

INDIVIDUAL GENIUS

GOVERNMENT

WAR

TECHNOLOGY

MONEY

The Industrial Revolution:
Surgery and Anatomy

Once more, there was another incredible change in the Industrial Revolution. More than 50% of patients died in surgery because of three main factors: pain, blood loss and infection. But this changed dramatically in the 19th century, and this started with surgeons gaining more respect. This meant they received more training, more hospitals sprung up and organisations (like the Royal College of Surgeons) were established to help and protect them.

John Hunter was an influential surgeon during this period. He was especially keen on the new scientific method (focussing on observation) and way of thinking. He amassed an enormous collection of anatomical specimens and made advancements in the knowledge of the structure of bones and teeth.

The issue of pain was resolved first. Prior to anaesthetics, the best surgeons required plenty of speed to ensure patients endured the pain of surgery for the least time, however, this obviously made surgery very dangerous. But in 1799 Humphrey Davy discovered laughing gas (nitrous oxide) which was mainly used by dentists. It reduced pain but did not knock patients completely out making it largely ineffective for bigger operations.

The second anaesthetic was called ether and was found by Crawford Long in 1842, and it was brought to Britain by Robert Liston. It was more effective but irritated the lungs of patients, was mildly explosive and made them vomit.

The most successful anaesthesia was chloroform; it was created in 1847 by James Simpson. He had been investigating different chemicals when he discovered chloroform which was powerful enough to knock patients out. This discovery was made through careful scientific research, as he would test chemicals with friends every evening to see if any would have any effect on them. His willingness to experiment set him apart from other physicians and scientists at the time.

He first tested it on a woman giving birth, and it worked rather well. Although there was much opposition to the use of it because it sometimes caused vomiting and often left a horrid taste in the mouth. It was also new and untested and furthermore anaesthetics didn't make surgery any safer (more advanced operations now carried out meant more deaths). Concerns were raised about easing the pain of childbirth (it was considered not natural, so God may get angry), and people felt pain was sent by God, so should be endured.

This opposition was overcome when chloroform was used by John Snow for Queen Victoria's last two childbirths.

In the 1880s and '90s, there was a so-called *black period* where its use was temporarily stopped because some patients died from its use. In general, it is quite a dangerous drug with dosage especially hard to control. Too much and the heart would stop beating. Longer-term it was found to cause liver damage and was replaced in the early 1900s by more effective injected anaesthetics which were pioneered by Helmuth Wesse. These injected anaesthetics allowed dosage to be controlled and thus making surgery safer.

The biggest killer in Industrial Revolution surgery, however, was an infection. Two individuals, Ignaz Semmelweis and Joseph Lister, played vital roles in changing that.

In 1847, Semmelweis was working in one of Vienna's hospitals when he noticed a trend between two maternity wards.

In one, where trainee doctors acted as midwives, there was a much higher death rate of pregnant mothers and new-born babies from childbed fever than in the other ward where just nurses were midwives. The trainee doctors regularly worked in the hospital mortuaries, and Semmelweis postulated that they transferred the diseases from the dead bodies to the wards.

He decided to insist that doctors should wash their hands in-between visiting the mortuary and ward, and it did cut the death rate. However, it did not last long for he was thought of as being completely mad. He had no proof; there was no Germ Theory, yet. People still, incredibly, felt an imbalance of humours or miasma (the existence of bad air) caused illness, so could not understand how they could transfer disease from a dead body to a live body. Although many doctors were willing to experiment with hand washing, they refused to believe Semmelweis' key idea: illness was caused by dirt alone.

In 1867, Joseph Lister was reading through Pasteur's Germ Theory and he thought these *germs* may have been the cause of *hospital fever* which was causing 50% of patients to die in, and after surgery. He set about to find a chemical that could kill these *germs*.

He'd heard how carbolic acid had been used to treat sewage and pondered whether it would be good for treating the wounds in his theatre. So, he first tested it on someone's broken leg, and the patient contracted no infection and didn't die. He was, therefore, the pioneer of antiseptic surgery. Before this, many doctors actually took pride in how dirty and stained their outfit was!

He decided to spray his whole theatre and all of his tools, and washed his hands in a 5% solution of carbolic acid;

he cut infection (and death rates) from 50% to just 15% in only 4 years.

Like many other important discoveries, he also faced much opposition. For starters, many surgeons didn't believe in Germ Theory and carbolic spray irritated their skin. Using carbolic spray made operations slower and more expensive. Furthermore, Lister was a poor public speaker, so struggled to promote it. He also kept changing his methods to improve them – some took this to mean he was wrong.

He was able to overcome his opponents by showing how the death rate in his operating theatre had fallen to as low as 5%, and then he was aided by research completed by Robert Koch showing that specific bacteria *did* cause specific diseases.

Aseptic surgery was an improvement on Lister's antiseptic. Aseptic aimed at preventing any germs from entering the operating theatre at all, instead of allowing them in and then destroying them with an antiseptic. In 1889, William Halsted in the USA pioneered it by introducing hats, gloves and gowns for surgeons. He emphasised the need for complete sterility. Also around this time, Robert Koch showed that equipment could be sterilised by using hot steam. In the 1890s hospitals were began to be rigorously cleaned.

Another important discovery occurred in 1895 because of a physicist Wilhelm Röntgen. He accidentally discovered X-Radiation (so called because it was an unknown quantity, so called it x as in maths where an unknown value in algebra is often labelled x) which, today, more commonly known as X-Rays. This was to have enormous benefits for the future.

Summary

- 3 Problems
- Pain: many died of shock. Laughing gas + ether, neither effective.
- 1847 James Simpson discovers chloroform. 1857 uses for Victoria. Black period 80s and 90s where many patients died + usage stopped.
- Joseph Lister 1854 develops carbolic acid – 1st antiseptic. Reduced death rate dramatically. Later aseptic surgery.
- 1895 Wilhelm Röntgen – X-Radiation

Factors

INDIVIDUAL GENIUS

TECHNOLOGY

GOVERNMENT (monarchy)

LUCK

WAR

The Industrial Revolution:
Public Health

Contrary to the rest of medicine, public health in the UK saw an unimaginable regression during the early part of the Industrial Revolution. Between 1750 and 1900 the size of towns and cities grew enormously because there were now many more jobs in the new factories and *industry*. The rapid urbanisation was far too quick for the Government to control, and as a result, some terrible public health issues arose. The Government would not have intervened anyway, as it followed a traditional Laissez Faire attitude which meant it would not becoming involved in the people. The public agreed with this notion.

Many more houses were built to cope with this rising population, however, landlords wanted to make the most profit, and therefore they built poor quality homes which were not maintained. To make matters worse, due to Laissez Faire approach, there were no regulations regarding house building.

There were no sewers, and waste was strewn onto the streets or dumped into rivers which were also used for drinking and washing. Houses were overcrowded – often tens of people to a room – and often hundreds shared just one toilet.

Air quality was also appalling. Factories released poisonous gases, and the narrow streets meant there was very poor ventilation. This contributed to many lung and respiratory problems.

Throughout the 19th-century things did slowly begin to improve, in part because of the hard work of some key individuals...

In 1837 birth and death records had begun being kept. This helped a man named William Farr who was first able to prove there was a link between living conditions and the death rate of an area. He showed how towns were unhealthier than the countryside, and he was able to prove how population density affected the death rate. He took a deep interest in the statistical information offered from the data; he set out to determine in great detail the causes of death of as many of the people who died as possible. He mapped London to show where, how and the age and sex of the people who died. He thought of some areas as healthy districts. Other unhealthy districts should aspire to be like these healthy districts.

Edwin Chadwick was a social reformer who published a report in 1842. In it, he discussed the living conditions in towns and pointed out that the poor in the countryside lived longer than the rich in towns. He thought that disease was the main cause of poverty.

He believed that by improving the health of the poor fewer would claim relief funds (small amounts of money from councils), thus saving the country money. He did all the research at his own expense.

He recommended that drains and sewers were improved, waste was removed from the streets, there was a medical officer for each town and that everybody had access to clean water facilities. This encouraged Parliament to think up a new set of laws, but in 1847 the Government voted *against* a new public health act. They were nicknamed the *dirty party* as a result. They rejected it because a) they didn't want to increase taxes, b) their Laissez Faire attitude and c) there was no proof of the cause of disease – no Germ Theory yet.

However, in 1848 the disease cholera (which will be discussed later) returned and Government, scared, rushed a new public health act through parliament. It said councils could set up a Board of Health, could connect houses to sewers and water pipes and could raise taxes to pay for it. It was a voluntary system. However, if the death rate was above 23 in every 1000 then a Board of Health had to be established, and the act became compulsory. Also, a National Board of Health was established in London, with Chadwick as its chairman.

This was the first time Government had accepted any responsibility for the health of its people and the Act finally challenged the Laissez Faire attitude of the time. Public health was now a national issue and remained regularly in the news. Furthermore, 2500 miles of sewers were built because of it.

Despite this, it had some large failings. It wasn't compulsory, for starters, and only one-in-six people were covered by a Board of Health. Many councils simply ignored the Act because of the cost. Mistakes were made, too. For example, Chadwick had insisted on waste being flushed into the Thames, used for drinking, which would have worsened the cases of many diseases including cholera. Chadwick was a difficult man to get on with, and he made many enemies; the effectiveness of the Act was, therefore, limited. When the National Board of Health shut in 1854 it essentially signalled the end of the Act.

Cholera was the most deadly disease in the Victorian era. Now we know it to be caused by polluted water. However, 200 years ago they thought it may have been because of miasma (bad and dirty air), God, or even those who lived *bad* lifestyles (i.e. drank too much alcohol). To try to combat it they set up quarantine hospitals, they released barrels of sulphuric acid to *clean* the air and people disinfected their homes – all of which did not work. However, they did clean up the streets which may have helped by reducing the possibility that pollution could have gotten into water supplies.

In 1854, John Snow worked out the real cause of cholera – dirty water – because he was very sceptical of the miasma theory. He produced detailed maps of London during an outbreak of cholera in Soho in 1854 showing how all the cases centred around one particular pump in Broad Street. He, therefore, inferred that this water pump, and subsequent dirty water, was causing cholera. He proved himself correct with three pieces of evidence.

The first stemmed from removing the handle of Broad Street water pump. After removing the handle (meaning it couldn't be used anymore), there were no more deaths in the area. Secondly, an old lady who used to live near Broad Street, but no longer did, died of cholera. She was the only person in her area who did so. He found out, that because she liked the taste, she had her water brought to her specifically from the Broad Street pump. Thirdly, nobody who worked in the Broad Street Brewery died, and he discovered that that was because they had their own water supply which was not the same as from the contaminated Broad Street pump.

Despite the conclusive evidence that cholera was caused by dirty, polluted water, he struggled to convince other doctors for they were certain it was miasma.

Towards the latter end of the 19th century, public health took a massive turn for the better. This was mainly due to the 1875 Public Health Act, and the events that preceded it.

It started in the summer of 1858: the year of the Great Stink. It had been very hot and dry, and the Thames began smelling so badly that even Parliament had to be abandoned! This convinced Government they had to act. Additionally, there were constant recurring instances of cholera, killing tens of thousands at a time.

Therefore, the government employed Joseph Bazalgette to build a new London sewer system to try and funnel waste away from the river. This acted as a trial for Government, to see whether paying for public health improvements would reduce disease and consequently death. It was officially opened in 1865 and was a technological marvel with nearly 1500 miles of sewers directly under London's streets. The plans for this were devised by Bazalgette. He worked obsessively over the plans to ensure every last detail was correct. As a result, his health unfortunately suffered.

He was very forward thinking, as he built the sewer's diameter much larger than it needed to be in order to cope with future population growth. In fact, his sewers are still in operation today. His sewers drastically reduced cholera outbreaks in London. The Governmental trial was very successful and helped to convince Parliament that public health measures did indeed work.

Prominent campaigners piled pressure on the Government to make changes. One such person was Octavia Hill. She bought 2000 slum homes and rebuilt them to a much higher standard – renting them at very reasonable prices. She also worked on improving life quality by introducing social facilities to these new residences. She had a major impact on the 1875 Artisans' and Labourers' Dwellings Improvement Act. Basically, this enabled local councils to destroy slum housing and rebuild them to better standards on health grounds.

Louis Pasteur's Germ Theory showed that dirt meant disease. This encouraged people to want to pay higher taxes for better health care. Opponents could no longer claim the money would be wasted.

In 1866 cholera returned which, again, scared people into action. The 1867 Reform Act gave an extra 1,000,000 men the vote (more of whom were working class). Before, only the upper class voted who didn't want to pay higher taxes to pay for public health. The new poorer voters expected more from their Government in terms of healthcare.

Back to the 1875 Public Health Act. It was compulsory, all councils HAD to provide clean water, sewers and drains whilst also having to appoint a medical officer of health to inspect conditions. Furthermore, the government banned the building of poor quality, slum housing by contractors. It also meant all roads had to be paved and contain street lighting.

Around the same time, many other laws came into effect. The maximum working hours for children were shortened, a ban on river pollution was introduced, housing regulations improved and education was made compulsory to name but a few.

Miscellaneously, in 1853 the soap tax was removed meaning more could afford it. Additionally flushing toilets emptying straight into the sewers were invented (however they were only affordable to the rich).

Summary

- The rapid expansion of towns due to the new industry (and jobs) in factories. Too quick for Government to control. No laws or regulations
- Massive decline in PH – crowded and air quality terrible
- Cholera massive killer – thought God, miasma or lifestyles. 1854 John Snow discovers real cause – Broad Street.
- 1837 birth and death records – William Farr (link between living standards and death rate)
- 1842 Chadwick produces a report on living conditions in towns – poor in the country live longer. 1847 PH Act is not passed: money, laissez-faire, no proof
- 1848 cholera returns – new PH Act. Not compulsory: board of health, the national board of health, sewers + water.
- 1858 Great Stink and Bazalgette – Governmental test is successful

- 1861 Germ Theory provides MPs with evidence
- Octavia Hill – slum housing + 1875 Artisans Dwelling Act
- 1866 Cholera returns
- 1867 – Reform Act and poor given vote
- 1875 PH Act is compulsory – and includes a medical officer

Factors

GOVERNMENT

TECHNOLOGY

MONEY

INDIVIDUAL GENIUS

LUCK

PART FOUR

Modern Times: *Disease and Infection*

The successes of the Industrial Revolution were continued into modern times (1900 onwards). From the late 1800s, scientists knew about the body's antibodies – our natural defence mechanism – and how they attacked specific pathogens. But, up until 1909, nobody had been able to create a synthetic version; a chemical that could cure somebody who already had a disease.

Paul Ehrlich had been a member of Robert Koch's team who were looking into staining bacteria so they could be easily seen under a microscope. He began looking for a dye that not only stained bacteria but also destroyed it. He was desperate to discover a *magic bullet* – a chemical which would zone in on the harmful pathogens and destroy them but harm no human tissue in the process. At this time, German chemical companies were improving rapidly which greatly helped him.

Ehrlich had already tested 605 arsenic-based chemicals on the bacteria that caused syphilis when the next one, the

606th, worked. He called it Salvarsan 606. However, as usual, there was some opposition to its use because it was painful to inject and, rather weirdly, some feared it would encourage promiscuity.

The second chemical cure was developed in 1932 by Gerhardt Domagk: Prontosil. He had been inspired by Ehrlich's work, and he had wanted to find a second magic bullet. Prontosil treated blood poisoning by preventing the disease carrying pathogen from multiplying in the body. He first tested it on mice and it had worked. However, he did not believe it would be effective on humans.

Soon after his discovery his daughter suddenly fell ill because she had cut her finger on some laboratory equipment. With no hope of survival, Domagk used his Prontosil as a last gasp attempt to save her. She survived, however, her skin did turn bright red!

With a new electron microscope developed in the 1930s, Prontosil could be analysed to find the active ingredients which made it work. It turned out to be sulphonamides; these are found in coal tar. They were good at curing many diseases, and so drug companies invested millions in finding more. However, they did cause serious side-effects and were found to cause damage to lungs, liver and kidney. Furthermore, they didn't actually have any effect on the stronger microbes.

The next great, albeit accidental, discovery was made by Alexander Fleming in 1928. While working in a World War 1 hospital he became interested in how living organisms could kill bacteria. He was well known for having a very messy office. In 1928, he was investigating bacteria when he accidentally left a petri dish full of bacteria open. Without him noticing, penicillin mould had gotten in. When he looked at it again later, incredibly he saw that the penicillin had killed the bacteria surrounding it. He had found the first antibiotic.

This *mould juice* was not pure (not as effective), although it could still cure many diseases. It came as an improvement over magic bullets, though, as it caused no damage to any human tissue. Nobody provided him with any funding due to the impracticalities of producing it on a large scale. He seemed to lose interest, moving on to other medical ideas. He published a report into his findings...

His papers were read by two men, Howard Florey and Ernst Chain, in 1937. They decided to pursue it further – to make it into a commercial drug. When World War 2 started, the UK Government donated a small amount of money, but UK drugs companies were too involved in the war effort to provide any assistance. Via a method known as freeze drying, they managed to create enough penicillin to test it on mice in 1940, and it was successful. By 1941 they had enough to test on a human being (he was a policeman). He had a very serious head injury, but the penicillin mould dramatically improved his condition, that is until it ran out and he died. It *did* prove, however, that penicillin mould definitely had a place in human medicine.

In 1942 they moved their work out to America (who were by now in the war), and the US Government paid drugs companies $80 million to mass produce penicillin. In 1943 the UK followed suit. By D-Day (6th June 1944), enough had been made for all the allied troops (2.3 million doses) and experts estimate its use saved an extra 15% of soldiers from dying.

After the war cheaper, faster and more effective methods of producing penicillin were created. However, in modern times bacteria are increasingly becoming anti-bacterial resistant leading to deadly *superbugs*.

The last great single discovery in the history of *Disease and Infection* came in 1953, courtesy (mainly) of two individuals: James Watson and Francis Crick. They discovered the double-helix structure of DNA and how it manages to replicate itself.

The discovery came about because they had substantial funding which afforded them the latest in technological advances (new microscopes, x-ray photography...) and many highly skilled engineers and technicians. Their team was vital to the discovery; one member, Rosalind Franklin, was the first person to photograph individual strands of DNA, for example.

The work on DNA led to many new advances and treatments in medicine, for example early screening for cancer, the ability to repair cells damaged by genetic diseases and the creation of genetic engineering (new plants which produce more food or bacteria which produce human insulin (for diabetes)). However, the new work on DNA has raised serious ethical issues with regard to *meddling* with nature.

Between 1986 and 2001 the Human Genome Project worked to extensively map out the function of every single human gene. James Watson was the professor in charge of this during its early formation.

On a side note, since World War 2 there's been an explosion in the amount of money spent by large drug companies in the field of research and development of new drugs.

Summary

- Paul Ehrlich looks for a dye that cures as well as stains. 1909 finds Salvarsan 606. However opposition: painful and promiscuous
- 1928 Penicillin – Alexander Fleming, LUCK. Impracticality and no funding = he leaves it. Published report.
- 1932 – Prontosil – Gerhardt Domagk. Tests on mice and dying daughter, turning her red.
- 1930s Electron microscope, discovers sulphonamides are the active ingredient. Investment to find more – side

effects: damage to liver, lungs and kidney. Don't work on strong microbes.
- 1937 Florey and Chain read AF paper. The UK give money, but chemical companies too caught up in war. USA – mass produced $80m. The UK then as well. Saves 15% at D-day.
- 1953 – DNA, James Watson and Francis Crick: cancer screening, genetic engineering, repairing cells damaged by genetic disease

Factors

TECHNOLOGY

MONEY

INDIVIDUAL GENIUS

LUCK

GOVERNMENT

WAR

Modern Times: *Surgery and Anatomy*

Again, during the 20th century more very important changes took place. Up until 1900, two of the three main problems with surgery had been solved: pain and infection. The last one, blood loss, was finally solved in 1901 by Karl Landsteiner.

From the 1880s surgeons had been attempting blood transfusions, however many died in the process. Landsteiner worked out why. He discovered that humans have different blood groups (A, B, AB and O), and that somebody had to have their same blood group transfused to them, otherwise they were poisoned, and their blood cells destroyed. After this, transfusions occurred with much greater success; the first one took place in 1907. However, the donor and patient had to be present at the same time – limiting its effectiveness. Every time blood was stored, it clotted and could not be used.

Even so, Landsteiner was essential in showing how blood transfusions should occur.

World War 1

The War had an enormous effect on surgery. The enormous number of injuries gave surgeons plenty of practice.

Furthermore, in times of war surgeons worked together, instead of competing against one another meaning change happened quicker.

War, it seems, always acts as a catalyst for change, and, due to large volumes of blood required, a method for storing blood was created making transfusions much easier and convenient. It was in 1914 that Albert Hustin worked out that by adding sodium citrate to blood it wouldn't clot, therefore it acts as an anticoagulant.

The use of X-Rays in a medical sense drastically increased, too, by virtue of the fact there were so many horrific injuries, so again war acted as a catalyst. Furthermore, a portable machine was created which could be used on the front. It helped surgeons find otherwise fatally lodged bullets and shrapnel, consequently saving many lives.

The field of plastic surgery was essentially pioneered by Harold Gillies. He invented the *tube pedicle* method by which new skin was grown in a tube attached to the patient and was then transferred to the required place on their body. He conducted some of the world's first skin grafts. This method improved on earlier French methods as it reduced infection rates. He carried out over 11,000 operations in a purpose built hospital in Sidcup from 1917. This hospital had more than 1000 beds, and most of the injuries treated stemmed from gunshot wounds.

Other minor improvements included a new way to treat broken bones, new techniques to reduce some infections (cutting away damaged tissue and soaking in saline – useless against serious infections) and better eye, throat, ear and nose surgery.

However, due to the huge numbers of soldiers who needed treating, surgeons had to work very fast. This meant they often had to revert to old fashioned and less effective methods of treatment to rapidly treat all the soldiers in their care.

During World War 2 Archibald McIndoe (cousin of Harold Gillies) made further improvements to plastic surgery. He worked in a hospital in East Grinstead founding a centre for plastic surgery. The serious burn injuries, caused by the new aviation warfare, created a need for better reconstructive techniques. McIndoe focussed on the psychological aspects of the treatments, and his patients nicknamed themselves 'The Guinea Pig Club'. He attempted to re-integrate his patients back into society in order to get them used to people seeing them as they were. He forced them to go to the pub and play local football matches all whilst the *tube pedicle* was still in place growing.

Also during World War II, Edwin Cohn developed a way of separating blood cells from the liquid plasma that surrounds it, this is called Blood Plasma Fractionation. This, like sodium citrate, ensured the blood did not clot, meaning it could be stored for later transfusion.

In 1946 blood transfusions improved again with the set-up of a National Blood Transfusion Service.

In the latter half of the 20th century organ transplantation developed enormously. In 1954 a kidney was transplanted between two brothers (only worked because they obviously both had very similar DNA). There was still a major issue of the body rejecting the donor organ, though. This was solved in 1959 when the drug *Imuran* was developed, which allowed the new organs to bypass the immune system. However, these immunosuppressant drugs left the body open and defenceless to other infections.

The most difficult transplant surgery (excluding the brain for obvious reasons) was always the heart. It was first successfully completed by Christiaan Barnard in 1967. However, the patient only lived for 18 days, dying from pneumonia contracted because of the immunosuppressant drugs.

He was helped by having a good team of nurses and anaesthetists, the latest technology (ECG and X-Ray machines), and the fact he was able to analyse blood chemistry and urine samples.

Despite this, nearly all the patients died very soon after heart surgery, and public opinion of it deteriorated quickly.

Despite Barnard's attempts to keep it going (by now he was seen as an enemy), its use was quickly stopped to be replaced by the use of artificial hearts in 1982.

Nearer to the modern day, further improvements to surgery have been made. Keyhole surgery means creating only a very small incision on the skin using fibre optics and an endoscope (reducing infection). This is popular amongst patients because there is only a small wound, and the recovery rate is much faster. Microsurgery allows surgeons to manipulate tiny blood vessels and nerves allowing limbs to be sewn back on. Lasers are increasingly being used in modern medicine: eye surgery using lasers can dramatically improve eyesight, for internal imaging of the body, and for cancer diagnosis and treatment (among many other uses).

Summary

- 1901 Karl Landsteiner discovers blood groups.
- WW1: a new method to store blood (separate cells OR add sodium citrate).
- 1895 Wilhelm Rontgen discovers X-Rays, use increases during WW1.
- Harold Gillies 1917 improved plastic surgery – skin grafts. For the first time he cared about how patient looked
- Archibald McIndoe – WW2. Worked on burned RAF pilots, realised they'd also need psychological support.

- Transplants: 1954 kidney, 1959 Imuran (bypasses immune system), 1967 Heart – Christiaan Barnard. He used a good team, ECG, X-Ray, blood chemistry and urine samples.
- Keyhole, micro and fibre optics.

Factors

WAR

TECHNOLOGY

MONEY

INDIVIDUAL GENIUS

Modern Times: *Public Health*

Despite the reforms of the previous century, many people still lived in poverty. It was only after the Government realised this that more changes began to take place.

Charles Booth was a businessman from Liverpool. In 1889 he went to live for several years with the poor in East London. He and his team extensively mapped every street (producing great coloured diagrams) creating a database of conditions, concluding that 35% of people lived in abject poverty. He recommended more governmental action, for example, to introduce an old age pension and free school meals for children; this affected later government policy.

However many didn't agree with him for they thought London was the exception, and that elsewhere fewer people lived in such conditions. Furthermore, contrary to what he seems to believe in, Booth was not a socialist. He only wanted these socialist reforms to be introduced because he felt they would make it less likely for there to be a socialist revolution, for he was very much capitalist in his views.

In 1901 Seebohm Rowntree (the sweet company) published a report called *Poverty: a Study of Town Life* about York. He was a very successful businessman. This was based on research he had conducted over the previous decade in which he had meticulously visited every single working class family, compiling data on 46,000 individuals. He discovered that 28% of people lived in poverty, helping to prove London was not alone in its problems. He believed in a poverty cycle. People were most at risk of abject poverty either when they were very old, or very young. He concluded that a low income was the root cause and not the traditional view of the upper classes that the poor were responsible for their own situation.

He increased his own workers' wages and published a new report in 1936 finding there'd been a 50% drop in poverty levels. Unemployment, he concluded, was the cause of any remaining poverty. He produced the third report in 1951 which showed absolute poverty had nearly been removed from York; it was now a rare exception. His influence was aided by the fact he was friends with David Lloyd George (who will be discussed later). He was influential in introducing an old age pension and the National Insurance Act.

The Boer War, 1899-1902, also highlighted to the Government how poor the state of the country's health was. Between 35-40% of recruits who volunteered were refused on medical grounds. In some towns, it was as many as 90%. Furthermore, during the war itself it took more than 400,000 professionally trained British soldiers three years to defeat 35,000 Boer forces, the poor fitness, condition and health of the soldiers were blamed. This revealed to the government that a huge number of the young men in the country were incredibly unhealthy.

In the 1906 General Election, the Liberal Party won a landslide victory. They won 214 more seats than they'd had at the previous election. They took drastic action, with the so-called *Liberal Reforms* to improve welfare led by Chancellor David Lloyd George and Prime Ministers Henry Campbell-Bannerman and Herbert Henry Asquith. This showed the final transition from laissez-faire attitude to the modern government we see today who involve themselves in the lives of the public.

The Liberal Reforms

Year	Reform(s)
1906	• *Local councils encouraged to provide free school meals for poorer children. This was made compulsory in 1914.*
1907	• *School medical checks introduced* • *Health visits to new mothers*
1908	• *Old age pension introduced for over 70s*
1909	• *Back-to-back housing banned*
1911	• *The National Insurance Act: scheme for workers to pay into. If they then couldn't work for some reason they would receive some money and could see a doctor free.*

In 1909, Lloyd George and Winston Churchill created the People's Budget, and this was passed by Parliament in 1910. This aimed to redistribute wealth by substantially increasing the taxation on the rich to pay for the welfare of the poor.

These reforms were successful, however, there were some limitations. National Insurance did not apply to women, children or the unemployed and the reforms did nothing to combat existing slum housing.

During the inter-war period, there were also some minor changes. In 1919 a new Housing Act (Homes fit for heroes - the soldiers) was introduced by the then Prime Minister Lloyd George. This provided new good quality council houses at affordable rates for the returning soldiers (and others).

However, in 1928 the Wall Street Crash set public health back. The Government had less money to spend and more people were unemployed (removing them from National Insurance) and couldn't afford to see a doctor. At this time there was a return to herbal remedies. The infant mortality rate increased, and the life expectancy of people decreased during this period.

World War 2

A series of minor advancements occurred as a result of World War 2. Firstly, the Government wanted a healthy nation to continue with the war effort, so more time and money was invested to ensure health improved. Funnily enough, rationing actually improved the diets of many of the poorer people, and the public propaganda posters gave valuable health tips. Furthermore, the Government organised a national diphtheria immunisation campaign.

The war acted as a social leveller – everybody was in the same predicament, and everyone was 'in it together'. The rich families who evacuated children were shocked as to how bad the condition of the evacuees was, and they began encouraging more change from the Government.

In 1942 William Beveridge published the Beveridge Report (he had been commissioned by the Government) about how to make Britain better after the war. He identified the 5 Giant Evils of society as *ignorance, squalor, idleness, disease,* and *need*. It had an enormous impact on the population, being bought more than 600,000 times, and being read many more times than that. He made many recommendations, including introducing a welfare state, increasing the scope of National Insurance to those not in work, and introducing a National Health Service (the NHS – to remove the disease aspect).

In the 1945 General Election, Labour crushed the other parties, and in that same year created a Family Allowance (essentially like child benefit).

Then in 1948 Labour began implementing plans for the new NHS; however, they faced a lot of opposition to it. Doctors thought they'd earn less and have their freedom taken away if they lost their private patients and the rich didn't want to pay higher taxes. Furthermore, local councils didn't want to lose control of their hospitals. But, through hard work by the health minister, Aneurin Bevan, (he told doctors they could work for NHS *and* have private patients) 90% of doctors had signed up by the 5th July 1948, when it officially began operating for the public.

The NHS was very popular, receiving millions of users in its first year. However, over time it's faced increasing difficulties and pressures regarding its budget. This is especially so in recent years with the new costs of advanced technology. Around 1950, charges were introduced for false teeth, glasses and prescriptions (and still remain today), and as a result Bevan resigned from the cabinet. As he allowed doctors to see patients privately, there still remains a divide between the services for the rich and for the poor.

Later, in 1956, a Clean Air Act was passed to help combat the smog in cities. Additionally, in the coming years, laws were created to ensure the cleanliness of water, that sewage was disposed of properly, toxic waste was dealt with appropriately and to make sure the hygiene standard of food remained high.

In the latter half of the 20th century, public health has continued to change. Now, the government plays a more active role. They run advertising campaigns to alert and inform the populace about health issues and run regular vaccination programs to prevent the outbreak of infectious disease.

Lung cancer became an enormous public health issue through the 20th century, probably as a result of an increase in the number of people smoking. In recent years, the trend has reversed and the number contracting the disease has decreased. With a greater awareness of the risks involved with smoking, fewer now smoke, and the cancer rates have likewise decreased.

Summary

- *1889 – Charles Booth report in London (35% of working class in poverty). People thought this would only be the case in London.*
- *1889-1902 Boer War highlights poor health as 30% recruits refused entry.*
- *1901 Seebohm Rowntree produces a report (Poverty: A Study of Town Life) about York – proves not just London (finds 28% in poverty). He is friends with Lloyd George. Increases his own workers' wages. 1941 new report finds 50% drop.*
- *1906 Liberal Reforms – school meals, health checks, pension, B2B housing, national insurance.*
- *1919 Homes fit for Heroes, 1928 Wall Street = recession = unemployed = no national insurance, 1930 Slum Housing Act*
- *WW2: Beveridge Report (1942), immunisation, posters, evacuation, rationing, healthy soldiers.*

- *1948 NHS: free healthcare. Initially doctors thought less money and rich higher taxes.*
- *1950 charges for prescriptions, dentist and opticians.*

Factors

GOVERNMENT

INDIVIDUAL GENIUS

MONEY

WAR

TECHNOLOGY

GOOD LUCK IN YOUR EXAMS!
Jack Hartell

Printed in Great Britain
by Amazon